Solitary Moonbeams

Lynn Kowal

PAGE PUBLISHING, INC.
New York, NY

First originally published by Page Publishing, Inc. 2017

ISBN 978-1-64082-353-2 (Paperback)
ISBN 978-1-64082-354-9 (Digital)

Printed in the United States of America

For Sara, my angelic muse

CONTENTS

PRIMAVERA

The wind moaned in the branches

As the sky released its starlings

Is it true what they say:

The first green of spring is gold?

The willows wept when they told me so.

The tulips shivered along the banks

Where the grass met the flowing stream

Reflecting pink and yellow and red in the dark blue water

The colors moving, swirling, carried on the powerful current

Fed by melting snow from high in the mountains above.

And the willows' leaves shone gold

In the rays of the setting sun.

ETERNAL REST

Bells rang in the distance
Imposing a sense of order
On this gilded space
Split open by the rapier spire
Of a white New England church
Notes that fields in the distance echoed
And mountains farther still, sent back
In waves that knew no bounds and
Found no sandy shore
On which to rest their languid tones,
Lay flat their ancient bones.
Yet behind the ivy-covered walls
Among the mossy churchyard stones
Is where they finally settled down
And where they found repose.

CHRISTO AND JEANNE-CLAUDE

I've always regretted not having seen *The Gates*

Not having witnessed the colorful fabric, billowing in the breeze

Not having sauntered beneath those saffron panels, enjoying Central Park in a new light.

And now she's gone or did he pass away?

I no longer recall.

Perhaps they're both creating art in a different dimension

Responsible for designing celestial patterns

Using clouds and reflected sunlight

As an ethereal palette to take our breath away.

THE AFFAIR

"Well, it's very French, you know," Monique responded
When I told her Jean-Luc had spent the night
French or not, he's married and this cannot be right.
"Oh, but it's so romantic!" Monique remained enthusiastic.
Yes, it was and I could not deny that I adored him so
But this was not my idea of the perfect mate.
Holidays and weekends would not be ours to share
Stolen hours, all we'd have; it was more than I could bear.
Yet the alternative was unthinkable…
Oh, why had I gone to the market on that cold February day?
Had I just stayed at home, I would not have seen
Jean-Luc's dark, wavy locks, handsome smile turned my way
As we considered artichokes, radishes, and Camembert.
We both made our way to check out, a fatal mistake
Waiting in the queue together, we talked of Arthur Rimbaud,
Rousseau, and Baudelaire
A philosophical debate, a meeting of the intellect,
Suffused with physical attraction that could not be denied.
We took the same Métro: Châtelet to Tuileries
We said "au revoir," knowing that there was more to come,
Knowing that we could not stay apart; we were destined to be together
We had no choice in the matter.
His lips briefly brushed my cheeks as we ascended to the boulevard
We went our separate ways, promising to meet
On the Champs-Élysées, we said—George V on Thursday for a drink
Then let destiny take its course…
From that point forward, I simply carried on

Waiting impatiently for Thursday
Oh, when would that day arrive?
The week was interminable—
Monday slowly sauntered past
Tuesday was difficult, but finally reached an end
Wednesday, a veritable frenzy, quickly moved ahead
Then Thursday dawned with a pink glow—was this an omen, I wondered,
Quickly dressing for work.
I plodded through the day, George V never leaving my mind.
Finally it was time for the appointed rendezvous
Grabbing a scarf, I hurried from my flat
Only then did I begin to worry:
> Would he remember my name?
> Would his smile be just as sexy?
> Would he still look as slim and tall?
> Would he even be there at all?
My fears were all allayed as the red awning of George V came into view
And Jean-Luc rushed out to meet me,
Held me tight and whispered my name.
A glass of wine turned into two
And evening became night
Although it was hard to say adieu
We managed just the same,
But not without making arrangements to see each other again.
Sometimes we'd meet at noon
Others under starlit skies
In flower-filled parks and in our cars
On bike paths along the Seine
We wandered through the Louvre and the Musée Marmottan
We met at cafés and bistros
"Sans Souci" near the Place des Vosges was among our favorite haunts
We walked beneath the Tour Eiffel, glittering in the night
We embraced life and love—
We embraced each other in those purloined moments,

Treasuring our time together,
As the weeks and months flew past.
But that was years ago and I have since moved on
I still call Paris home but now have a country cottage
As I told Monique, it's on the coast, near le Mont Saint Michel
And, as you drive along the back road, look for the sign near the gate
"Sans Souci" it's called
"Sans Souci," I repeated as her mobile faded in and out
Looking from the upstairs window, I glimpsed her old Renault
Creeping slowly down the lane, now turning in the gravel drive
Jean-Luc walked out to meet her, our daughter running behind,
Dark curls flying in the wind, her doll clutched to her side.

YIN AND YANG

A sycamore grew in a clearing
On a cold winter day
Low clouds gave up flurries
White and fluffy they fell
Circling the bare branches of that tree
Settling on its mottled bark
Wrapping it in a wintry cloak
Increasing its size twofold.

A blackbird flew in to this very white world
Presenting a stark contrast between darkness and light
Standing first on one foot, then the other
He mused on the meaning of life:
His thoughts were thunderous in the muffled quiet.

VANISHED

The coast was rugged,

Cloaked in fog.

A figure walked

Among the rocks.

Solitary, exuding loneliness,

Like an image from a Hopper painting.

The waves rolled in,

Erasing footprints from the sand,

Removing all traces of this man.

THE BEACH

It was a sun-burnished day,
One of the last of summer
And we lay on the sand, side by side.
The sky was blue—cloudless,
The waves gently lapped the shore.
I stole a glance at your profile,
Tanned skin silhouetted against the rocks,
Ray-Bans perched on your Roman nose.
I imagined your tattoo, discretely hidden,
Just below your swimming trunks
  "Resistance is futile" it read,
In neat Edwardian script.
With that, I could not disagree.

THE MERMAID

The mermaid emerged
From a Russian fairy tale
Riding the waves
Scales reflecting the sun
Silver and gold, overshadowed by blue,
The sea's sapphire depths
Azure tones of the sky
The tide rushed in
Drowning out the sounds of her cries
Too many secrets, too many lies
A crime of passion
Behind the louvered doors
Of the beach house
High above the dunes
Beyond the stepping stones
And the wave-lapped shore.

OCEAN LADY

Seaweed ensnared her ankles
As she waded deeper into the sound
The sand left an impression
On her toes
Or was it the other way round?
She no longer knew—she couldn't think clearly
The incoming waves assaulted her body
And her mind
She drew a deep breath—the air smelled of fish,
Of salt, of water, of sea glass—of sea glass?
Her senses were heightened, yet confused —they misled her:
She felt sights; she heard the viscosity of the sun-drenched water;
She tasted the torment of the sea; she smelled the thundering
Of the waves as they crashed against the shore.
She tumbled with them, oblivious to her direction,
Abandoning her soul to their relentless momentum
As they dragged her beyond the easternmost buoy
Beyond the last sandbar… beyond a reasonable doubt… beyond the
point of rescue
Yes, she thought, I am being pulled out to sea
But I refuse to put up a fight
I refuse to acknowledge my fate
I refuse… I refuse… I refuse
She felt the words bubble to the surface
She watched as they glistened in the light

And then the darkness closed in…
She could hear it as it arrived
She tasted its velvety cloak, surrounding her with night.

MY KITE

The wind sighed and let you go
  Off in the distance
    High as white clouds
      Over the dunes, toward the dark blue depths of the sea

Racing to reach a point just above…
              …above the grey gull's wing

Climbing to heights far beyond…
            …beyond all imagining

Just as you felt most free…
            …free of the ties that bind

The wind bid adieu and let you return
Back to the earth and to me.

What She Saw

She saw herself in the window,
A silhouette of remorse

Bare branches scratched
Against the roof

A vast expanse stretched out before her,
Endless in the night

The sky was dark and threatening;
Rain began to fall

She saw a laughing crowd,
A carafe of wine being passed

The language was not her own;
She did not share their mirth

She saw herself in the mirror,
A sadness etched on her soul.

SOMETHING MACABRE

Something macabre is in the air;
I can sense it in the way
The candles flare.

The curtains shift although there is no breeze;
The hairs on my neck
Tingle and then they freeze.

Footsteps can be heard on a distant floor,
As restless spirits wander
In search of the door.

It's All Hallows' Eve and jack-o'-lanterns shine bright
From each and every window
In the town tonight.

Ghouls and goblins traipse from door to door,
Asking for sweets
And nothing more.

But there is no doubt a sinister presence awaits
Those who dare venture
Beyond the city gates.

Something macabre is in the air;
I can see it in
The black cat's stare.

ASTROPHYSICS: THE JOURNEY

We sail forth through the heavens
On this blue-encrusted orb
Never doubting our path,
Nor flinching from our course.

Bending space-time as we travel
In a continuum of darkness
Toward an infinity unspoken
Forever expanding, unbounded and unbroken.

The gas giants in their places
Slowly plod 'round the sun
Gravity their master,
Beholden to none.

Orion watches over us
Steed and sword at the ready
To defend against the enemy:
An asteroid's destiny.

Though cosmic dust may cloud our view
As light-years unfold before us
We continue on, undaunted
Seeking other worlds, so glorious.

I Love You

I love you for all the men I never knew
I love you for all the time I never lived
For the unspoken secrets deep within my soul
For the bridges to infinity spanning out below
I love you for all the men I never loved

Who reflects me if not you; I see myself so little
Without you I see only a deserted expanse
Between another time and today
I could not pierce the wall of my mirror
I had to learn life word by word—how one forgets!

I love you for your knowledge which isn't mine
I love you above all that is only illusion
You believe yourself to be doubt and you are only reason
You are the great sun that rises in my head
When I am sure of myself

I love you forever
I love you for you.

THE CAFÉ

They say a madman wandered here
An aimless, wretched path of pain
Voices calling from near and far.

Is it not enough to see his work, so luminous
So full of life, of vibrant essence
Swirling hues, fantastically rendered?

Is it the color we recall?
The blue, the orange, the yellow true
Or some deeper resonance still?

Do the heavens touch our very souls?
Do the stars bear witness from above
To this most delicate love?

At a table now we'll rest
Sipping wine by candlelight
The world fades into nothingness…

Yet in one's mind, the scene is clear:
A tiled walk, a lantern bright
So many tables in the night.

Shuttered rooms lie sleeping up above
An awning shelters those below
While others stroll the cobbled streets.

Imagined footsteps in the night
Under starry, lantern light
Captured forever by his hand.

A life long o'er
Remembered still
On canvas signed and framed and hung.

They say a genius wanders here
Between the tables, ever near
Seeking understanding, seeking truth.

Composed as a tribute to Vincent Van Gogh and his painting *Café Terrace at Night*, 1888

THE PIRATE

Besotted fool, he strode away
The parrot watched him go
Red, yellow, green, and blue, he was—a carnival of color
And in a mocking tone he spoke:
"Goodbye, lad. Goodbye, lad. Bye-bye, laddie boy.
The girl's not yours. She's not yours. The girl's not yours tonight."
His boots were high and shiny black
Their heels made a ringing sound
With every step he took
That bore him farther afield,
Away from the girl that was not his; no, not his tonight.
He loved her dear and true, he did
His eye, it never wandered,
Never a fair maiden did he spy
Who could compare to the raven hair
Of the beauty he left behind.
He traveled the oceans deep and blue,
To exotic ports of call
He never strayed; his heart was true
To the bonny love he called his own
Waiting, always waiting, for him to come home.
And now he returned to hold her close,
To smell her perfumed breast,
To taste her tender lips and press
Her near, close against his chest.
But she was not his; no, not his—the girl was not his tonight.
He rushed ashore, hoping to find

His girl waiting there
Just as he'd left her late last year
Her passion burning bright.
But she wasn't there; she was no longer his; the girl wasn't his tonight.
He searched the fields high and low,
Hoping to find her there
To see the lace of her long skirt
A ribbon in her braided hair
To catch a glimpse of moonlight
Upon her skin so fair.
Alas, he could not find her
For they had no plans to meet
His ship had reached the dock early by a week.
And his girl wasn't waiting; she did not wait for him tonight.
After searching far and wide for her
His thirst more than he could bear
He stopped at a roadside tavern
For a pint of ale or two
And there at last he found her
On the ostler's lap she sat
Her arms around his neck; she laughed,
Caressed and held him tight.
For she was his; the girl was his; she was the ostler's girl tonight.

THE LAST ORCHID: A SEASONAL ODYSSEY

The last orchid bloomed;
Darkness fell—silent, brooding
Not allowing a glimmer of hope,
A sparkling of starshine, to cast its glow
To echo between snowcapped mountaintops
To reflect the frozen atmosphere
In myriad mirrors, an icy glare.

The last orchid bloomed;
No moon rose above the forest
To shine on spruces, oaks, and birches
To light a path among these woods
To show the way through fallen leaves
Illuminating all that breathes,
All that dwells within these trees.

The last orchid bloomed;
The velvet drapes of night o'erpowered
The sweetness of the summer breeze
Wrapping all within its fabric
Cloaking the fertile fields in black
Snuffing out the warmth of day
Letting nothing block its way.

The last orchid bloomed;
The springtime sky of pastel hue
Fell victim to the shadows
Advancing in the gloaming
Covering hills and valleys
Verdant fields of tender grasses
All were lost amidst the blackness.

The last orchid bloomed;
Darkness fell—silent, brooding
No moon rose above the forest
The velvet drapes of night o'erpowered
The springtime sky of pastel hue
The orchid flow'r was drenched in dew.

NON SEQUITUR:
SEVEN VIGNETTES

I

Fields of wheat were strewn with boulders
Placed there in the night
Like a giant's chess set
Or a suit of hand-me-down clothes
Oblivious to their owner, seeking only to exist
Without identity or a sense of purpose
Beyond the here and now
Accepting of their fate, they listened
For a nod of approval, a cue to carry on
A reason to be grateful, albeit extemporaneously.

II

The rope was incongruous with the crystals
Then again, my hands were incongruous with her neck
A fibrous blend of hemp and a brilliant spectrum of light
Glinting incandescently in the sun
Ivory and red, ivory and red, ivory and red and white
Tightening, constricting, the tinkle of shards of glass
Swarovski littered the ballroom
Extended into the hall
Beyond the marble foyer
Black and white tiles and all.

III

A long, low whistle approaching—
The train roared along the track
A marble statue appeared
In the center of a well-manicured lawn
And after dark she jumped down
From the pedestal that held her high
Above all the rest, beyond reproach
Into the deep blue sky
Head and shoulders surrounded by clouds
She climbed aboard the train, altering the Doppler effect.

IV

Fingerprints on beveled glass
The dog sat upright at the table
A full moon rose above purple mountains
The abuse continued in spite of the law
And the barking would not stop
A clown was juggling pumpkins
Along with several of Jupiter's moons
The red spot hid under the table
But was indifferent to the dog
And yet the barking continued; it simply would not stop.

V

We went to Paris in April
To experience springtime in all her glory
They told us there's nothing better
Than "avril" in the City of Light
And the coven of witches did not disagree
In fact, they expected us there
But we did not plan for a cat
Or green brooms on the doorstep at night
The Eiffel Tower made an appearance
But that was largely out of spite.

VI

He whistled as he walked through the doorway
And the cobblestones glistened in the mist
There was talk of mutiny on board
But that was exaggerated at best
Lights glowed in the tavern windows
While the King of Spades lay down to rest
On a bed of nails strewn with roses
Their petals pierced his heart
His blood ran red on the metal bed
And the clock struck the hour in the dark.

VII

A scream pierced the cold night air
Somewhere in Tehran a plume of smoke rose in the distance
A cow sneezed, causing a cosmic shift
In the dynamics of the whole barnyard
Is this chaos theory? Is it?
We did not expect her to wear a yellow dress
Although we knew the stilettos would be red
The farmer awoke from a sound sleep and sat bolt upright in bed
"Gesundheit," he murmured; "Gesundheit," he repeated
That was all he said.

ALL THE WORLD WAS STILL

We went for a walk one winter's eve

In the freshly-fallen snow;

The pine boughs glimmered and glistened,

And the world was all aglow.

Our footsteps were crisp as we made our way

By the light of a crescent moon;

Along a snow-covered forest path,

To the edge of an icy lagoon.

The wind was a howling monster

Out of the frozen north;

Our faces were red, and our hands were numb,

Begging return to warmth.

Yet onward we trekked in the darkness

Not giving in to the cold;

We passed the innkeeper's welcome light,

And continued on so bold.

We climbed the craggy, lichened rocks

To reach the top of the hill;

The town was nestled down below,

And all the world was still.

THE STORM

Too restless to stay seated,
Yet not energetic enough for calisthenics,
I paced from one end of the room to the other
As the wind howled down the chimney
And the rain beat against the windowpanes.
I could barely see beyond the marsh grasses
To the dunes being pounded by frothy grey waves.
The few boats moored just offshore rocked wildly,
As the storm battered them fore and aft.
A lone fisherman attempted to spread a tarp,
His yellow mac the only splash of color in this monochromatic world.
The gulls had been crying since early morning,
The first harbingers of the bad weather to come.
I should have driven inland, I realized now
For the coastal roads would likely flood,
Stranding me here for days on end; yes, days on end
Endless days, and even longer nights—
Long, dark nights devoid of companionship.
A banging began upstairs as a shutter broke loose
And hit the shingles, over and over, matching the cadence of the
wind.
The lights flickered and then went out.
The wind howled down the chimney,
And the rain beat against the windowpanes.
The gulls continued their cries,
And the coastal roads flooded over,
And over, and over again.

35

ARTEMIS

She wept in a field of flowers;
The petals fell like rain.
The wind stirred their stems,
Whispering her name.
Her sadness overwhelmed the garden,
Drenching all in pain.

Bright colors became muted,
Blended into grey.
Turned into night
What had begun as day.
Shifted the brilliant landscape
To a most desolate display.

Uprooted pink cleome,
Caused lavender to wither and fall.
Astilbe lost their vigor,
No longer standing tall.
And clematis, purple clematis,
Collapsed against the wall.

Yes, she wept in a field of flowers;
The roses felt her pain,
Their thorns transformed to weapons

Bloody stems, all that remain.
And the daisies—oh, the daisies,
Their petals fell like rain.

SAMOSIR ISLAND, SUMATRA

And for what reason, tell me do
Are their bamboo mansions built
Above the ground—on stilts, you say?
Yes, stilts, that's true, I do
Much closer to the gods they are
They mean no disrespect
To hover there, above the ground, you see
Just nearer heav'n than earth to be.
Outside each door a cage is placed.
A cage, you say?
I do, a pigeon cage to be precise.
The doors are never closed.
The birds can come and go, you see
Just as they please, it's true.
And so these birds, at liberty,
To feed and fly between
The gods and mortal man, they are
A kind of liaison, emissaries of sorts, I mean;
Yet they have another function too,
And that you cannot guess.
You're right, I will allow,
And ask you to reveal it, please.
Well, when a neighbor comes to call,
They are the doorbells here
To arouse those who dwell within;
So with their cooing sounds begin
To announce a guest's arrival

And summon those inside
To venture forth and greet
The one who at the door awaits
Entrance into that humble abode,
On stilts, you will recall,
To visit and enjoy a spell
Of Sumatran hospitality.

A-Muse-ing

A muse, they called her a muse,
But whom did she inspire?
Who wore the lederhosen
In these castles in the air?
Neither a continent nor an ocean
Could ever keep us apart.
We lit one hundred candles
Then watched them dispel the night,
Awaiting words of inspiration
Which she would not fail to provide.

Waves crashed on distant shores;
The wind howled through the valley.
Then she rose above the mountain
Blonde braids encircling her head,
Her gown a diaphanous white,
Her voice an angel's whisper
Declaring; no, rather questioning, "Chapter two?"
"Two?" we echoed through the canyons.
"Two!" came back to us;
Bounced from rock to rock,
From craggy peak to mountaintop.

Why not "One"? What had she done?
We could not begin *after* the beginning.
This was a travesty of the highest order;
To be so galvanized, yet skip so far ahead.

Was her genius now in question?
Her words beyond the pale?
This was passing strange, as she was wont to say,
Requiring more analysis,
More thought than we were prepared to give;
So we did not deliberate, did not pontificate;
We simply moved on…
"Chapter three," we wrote and laughed,
For this we found to be highly amusing.

EINE HALBE STUNDE

She knew they would arrive
In eine halbe Stunde
Eine halbe Stunde—a half hour
She enjoyed interspersing German
Words in her English thoughts
She relished the juxtaposition,
The different sounds, the looks
of incomprehension
for her friends did not understand
They found her bizarre,
eccentric in her misunderstood ways
She left her shoes by the door.

STRINGS ATTACHED

There was an expectation that we would behave
According to a predefined plan.
Although the evening was young,
Chairs tucked beneath linen-cloaked tables,
Set with glittering china and sterling,
Tapers as yet unlit; flowers still fresh in their vases
We knew the night was not our own
We were beholden to the puppet master
To guide our every move
To dictate words and even laughter
Our hands as they reached for the goblets
Skirts that rustled on the dance floor
All were orchestrated well in advance,
Planned to the nth degree.
In spite of ourselves, when we answered,
We knew we were not free,
Free to say "savoir faire" and not "cunning"
At liberty to stroll between tables
Conversing with Antoine, not Paul
No, it was not meant to be
We had a script to follow
To deviate would not be allowed
"Verboten" was the preferred term
So we went about our meal,
Assuming a nonchalance,
Contrived by its very essence
We passed serving platters

From one to another,
Speaking of inconsequential matters
Then suddenly we wondered:
Although our actions were monitored,
Could our minds be controlled as well?
A hush descended over the room,
And we thought what we wanted to.

TRIBAL STAGE

The boundary was indistinct
It was easy to slip inside
From the deep Atlantic waters
To the Indian spirit world,
A world of incandescent fire
Where dancers and medicine men cavort
About a stage that's set, and all are actors there
Playing parts assigned and roles designed
By the ancient Hopi men.
It was well-suited to your desires,
Aligned with your innermost goals
And now you're happy, yes, I see
Playing a role that was meant to be.

Composed in memory of JFK, Jr.
1960–1999

A VICTORIAN NIGHT

Her footsteps echoed on the cobblestones
As she made her way across town
The streets were empty; it was late at night
Fog rolled in from the sea
Gas lamps cast an eerie glow
There was little comfort from their light
She thought she saw a shadow
A slightly darker image,
Crouching off to the right
Yet she continued on in the darkness
And kept a steady pace.
Clutching her cloak tight to her throat,
She hummed a silly tune, a child's nursery rhyme:
"Goose-a goose-a gander... Whither shall I wander?"
Over and over she repeated the words, an incantation bright
But they did little to dispel the feeling,
The feeling that all was not right.
Her footsteps echoed on the cobblestones
She clutched her cloak tight to her throat
And continued on through the night.

I Said Yes

He asked if I would love him forever
And I said yes.

He asked if I would be his bride,
Whom he could carry across the threshold wide

He asked if I would stay close by his side,
With never a secret to hide

He asked if I would in his castle reside,
Content within those stone walls to abide

He asked if I would always consent to ride
His steed with the dappled hide

He asked if I would never deride
Mistakes he might make in his stride

He asked if I would love him forever
And I said yes.

A LAMENT

"A lament," she shrieked across the sand,
Each grain absorbing the words of torment.
"It's a lament upon the soul," she elaborated.
"The tortured wrath of barbarous wretches."
Fanned by the hot Namibian winds,
Her words seared into and under the skin
Leaving little room for other thoughts
Dominating the landscape of this desert
Sliding over the dunes,
To the sea beyond,
Echoing into the void,
Then returning to assault the senses again.

SPELLBOUND

We skipped our merry, sprightly way
Into the forest late that day
And in the gloaming far ahead
We glimpsed the glow of gypsies' fire
Sparks filled the air and music, too
From cimbalom the gypsies played.
Their brightly-colored caravan
Beyond the clearing near a stream
Embraced by willows' weeping branches
Reflecting firelight in its waters
Where the gypsies bathed and drank
Where the gypsies read tarot cards
And danced in circles, taking turns
Moving from one partner to another
With swirling skirts, long dark hair flying
Dusty boots on hard earth resounding
Golden earrings catching light,
As the gypsies danced tonight,
As the gypsies cast their spells.
We stopped and watched,
Entranced we were
By the music and the light:
Otherworldly became this night.
We tried to leave but lost our way
Moving in circles, always back
To the mystical firelight
Where the gypsies danced tonight.

We Used to Say Hi

All I can remember
Are the last words that he said
When he passed me in the hallway
As I was walking straight ahead.
"We used to say hi," he uttered.
And, yes, that was very true
We often exchanged greetings,
Followed by a word or two:
"The heatwave was just dreadful!"
"Interest rates on the rise…"
"And the latest troop deployment—
Do you think that was wise?"
Our paths still crossed from time to time,
Yet we no longer paused to talk.
Were we simply too busy,
Completely lost in thought?
Our eyes met, we nodded, but moved on silently,
As if we were strangers and
Words a costly commodity.
How did it come to this, I often wonder now—
I have not seen him since that moment
When he stopped me in the hall
With that succinct communiqué,
Words that haunt me to this day.

Imagining We Were Lovers

It began as just a game
Since I see you every day
Sometimes in the café for a "pain au chocolat"
Or later on the Métro as we make our way to work,
You in your leather jacket, me in my miniskirt.
We part ways at the Place Vendôme
You work for an art dealer there and I in the museum shop.
I think about you as I sell
Postcards of La Joconde,
Calendars depicting masters' works
Or medieval tapestry
And I wonder: do you think of me
As you go about your day
Selling antiquities: putti and busts of clay?
Later on the Métro home
You cross my mind again
Sometimes I see you there,
Others in my thoughts alone.
So I began to imagine
What it would be like
To actually be your lover
To hold hands as we ride the train,
Rest my head on your leather-clad shoulder,
Share an umbrella in the rain,
Enjoy croissants in my darkened flat
After a passionate night
Rather than in the café

At separate tables in bright sunlight.
But that is just a dream of mine
For at the end of the day
I know it will never happen
Since you are obviously gay.

WHATEVER BECAME OF THESE NOVEL CHARACTERS?

I spent many an intimate hour with you
Night after winter night
On the sofa by the fire
Reading about your exploits
Becoming entwined in your lives
Two sisters on a veranda in Venice
Who travelled to Italy in search of love
A blond DCI from Penzance
Who solved every case that came his way
The widow who moved to a seaside cottage
Then longed for tea with her friends in London
The artist struggling to survive
In a garret in southwest Paris
College roommates on a train to Rome
With high hopes for their spring holiday
A distraught couple whose autistic son
Was found drowned in a nearby lake
On and on the list continues
From all the books I've read
I think about you as I work
Tallying figures in my head
Sending email messages to colleagues
From California to Kuala Lumpur
Wondering what you're doing
While I'm so far away
Until each evening when I return
To resume our time together

But once the last page is turned
I cannot help but ask
What has become of you?

WHAT I WOULD DO IN SUMMER

In the depths of frozen winter
I contemplate Summer in all her glory
A beautiful muse with a colorful garland
Woven through her long blonde hair
I imagine walks in flower-filled parks
The scent of freshly-mown lawn in the air
I'd climb upon a swing, fly into the bright blue sky
Tanned limbs stretching to reach new heights
The wind rushing through my hair.
I'd pack a picnic basket filled with seasonal delights
Lush red strawberries and perhaps even apple pie
I'd plant flowers in all the gardens
Delphinium of the brightest blue
Poppies and iris and bee balm in every possible hue
I'd drive to the nearest beach
Down on the Rhode Island shore
And walk for miles in the sand
'Til I couldn't take any more
Then I'd lie on my towel and dream
I'd dream of a ski slope in winter
Flying along snowy trails
Fresh powder sparkling in the sun
My cheeks cherry red in the cold.

'TIL DEATH DO US PART

Everything is settled.
      The grave is ready.
Black, black as the night which
      dances irrevocably toward the
           light
We will be there; we will all be there
         together.
And then, the suspense… the apprehension
      Gleaming in the April sunlight… last glimpse
        of daylight
      And then, the descent…
      down
            down
                down
      Eternal Rest.
    Waiting, like the night… alone
Tears, like the early-morning dew glimmering
     One ray of white light
      Truth
Like the single white rose
   I left
   The grave,
      Peaceful.

ABOUT THE AUTHOR

Lynn Kowal lives and writes in southern New England.

Undergraduate studies in English and French literature have helped shape her writing style, while holidays in Europe continue to provide inspiration for her poems.

An ardent admirer of the arts, Lynn enjoys visiting museums throughout the world. She is especially fond of the Musée d'Orsay in her favorite city, Paris.